Mon Gets Six

By Sally Cowan

Mon and Kip got six nuts.

"Look, Kip!" said Mon.
"I can get six figs!
We can mix the nuts
and the figs.
Yum!"

"You can not get the figs," said Kip.

"This big log tips!"

"We can fix it!" said Mon.

Mon and Kip got a log.

"This log is on the big log," said Mon.

"I **can** get six figs!"

Mon ran up to get the figs.

But here is Vox!

Mon got wet!

He did not get six figs.

So Mon and Kip
had the six nuts.

Yum, yum, yum!

CHECKING FOR MEANING

1. How many nuts did Mon and Kip get? *(Literal)*

2. Where were the figs? *(Literal)*

3. Why did Mon go into the water? *(Inferential)*

EXTENDING VOCABULARY

yum	What does *yum* mean in this story? How many sounds are in the word? If you took away the *y* and put the letter *h* at the start, what word would you make?
fix	If you have to *fix* something, what do you do? What things have you had to fix? Can you think of other words that mean the same as *fix*?
Vox	How many sounds are in this word? What are they? Can you make a new word by changing the letter *V*?

MOVING BEYOND THE TEXT

1. What did Mon and Kip do in this story that people might do?

2. What do figs look like? Have you eaten a fig? What did it taste like?

3. Talk about the places where fruits grow. Which ones grow on trees and which ones grow on smaller plants?

4. What is your favourite fruit? Why?

SPEED SOUNDS

Xx	Yy	Zz

Kk	Ll	Vv	Qq	Ww
Dd	Jj	Oo	Gg	Uu

Cc	Bb	Rr	Ee	Ff	Hh	Nn
Mm	Ss	Aa	Pp	Ii	Tt	

PRACTICE WORDS

mix

six

fix

yum

Yum

Vox